homes
chinese
cooking

Daniel Reid

A selection of delicious Chinese dishes that are easy to prepare at home, and light and healthy too!

PERIPLUS

Basic Chinese Ingredients

Coriander leaves or cilantro are the leaves of the coriander plant and are often referred to as Chinese parsley. They have a strong flavor and aroma and are typically used as a garnish.

Dried black Chinese mushrooms are used widely in Chinese cooking. The dried mushrooms must be soaked in hot water to soften before use, from about 15 minutes to 1 hour,

depending on the thickness of the caps. The stems are removed and discarded; only the caps are used. Shiitake mushrooms are a good substitute. They are easily available from the dry food sections in wet markets and supermarkets.

Five Spice Powder is a highly aromatic blend of Sichuan pepper, cinnamon bark, clove, fennel and star anise, ground to a fine powder and used to season stir-fried foods, in marinades and for sauces.

Rice Wine is used frequently in Chinese cooking, as a tenderizer, to blend flavors and to enhance taste. The best wine for Chinese cooking is *hua diao* rice wine, Japanese sake or *mirin*. A good alternative is dry sherry.

Sesame Oil is extracted from sesame seeds that have been well toasted, producing a dark, dense, highly aromatic oil that can be used for cooking, marinades, sauces and soups, or as a table condiment. Its nutty, smokey flavor has become a hallmark of Chinese cuisine.

Sichuan Peppercorn is also known as *fagara*, Chinese brown pepper-

Dark Soy Sauce   Light Soy Sauce

Soy sauce is indispensable to Chinese cuisine. It is fermented from soya beans and salt; used in marinades, stir-fry cooking, sauces and dips; low-salt varieties are now available. It is well worth spending a little extra to purchase high-quality soy sauce, because its distinctive flavor permeates Chinese cuisine, and a poor quality soy sauce can ruin the taste of even the best cooked food. Both light and dark soy sauces are used in the recipes in this book.

Soft tofu

Firm tofu

Pressed tofu
(*Tau kwa*)

Deep fried tofu
(*Tau pok*)

Tofu or bean curd comes in various form. *Soft tofu* is silky and smooth. *Tau kwa* is hard tofu that has been compressed to expel most of the moisture. Small squares of **fermented tofu** are sold in jars. They are either red on the outside, if flavored with chilli and spices, or creamy white and used as a condiment with rice porridge. Another type of bean curd sometimes added to braised dishes or soups is dried-fried bean curd, *Tau pok,* which is generally sold in small rectangles. These are often sold on strings in Asia, but are elsewhere usually packed in plastic. They are light and spongy in texture, and need to be dipped briefly in boiling water to remove the oil before being used. Dried deep-fried bean curd has an almost nutty flavor and is particularly appreciated for the way it soaks up the liquid to which it is added. It can be kept refrigerated for at least two weeks.

corn and flower pepper. This spice has a sharp pungence that tingles and slightly numbs the lips and tongue, an effect known in Chinese as *ma la* (numb hot).

Sichuan Pepper-salt Powder may be prepared by toasting 2 tablespoons Sichuan peppercorn in a dry pan with 1 teaspoon sea salt, grinding them to a fine powder, and sprinkling the powder over cooked dishes; the peppercorns are also used whole in spice bags for stews.

Tofu Skin is the thin layer of soy protein that forms on top of soybean milk when it is boiled. The skin is skimmed off and dried. It is sold in sheets as a wrapper, or as *tau fu kee*, a thick twisted skin added to meat or vegetable dishes. It has little flavor but a wonderful texture. It is to be moistened with a wet cloth before use. It is a widely-used ingredient in vegetarian foods as it is a good and healthy alternative to meat. Tofu

skin can be deep fried, steamed or even used as a garnish.

Vinegar is used to balance flavors in sauces and to bring out the natural tastes of foods, almost always in conjunction with a bit of sugar. Unless the recipe calls for a specific variety of Chinese vinegar, the best choices are rice vinegar or apple cider vinegar. Red wine vinegars do not go well with Chinese flavors.

Wasabi is one of the best known of all Japanese condiments. It is a very spicy Japanese horse-radish that is sold in powdered form or as a prepared paste.

Poached Tofu with Spicy Sauce

2 liters (8 cups) water
250 g (9 oz) medium
  or firm tofu
1 tablespoon garlic,
  minced
1 tablespoon ginger,
  minced
3 spring onions, minced
1 sprig fresh coriander
  leaves (cilantro), minced

Sauce
1 tablespoon sesame oil
1 tablespoon chilli oil
1 tablespoon soy sauce
1 teaspoon black pepper
$^1/_2$ teaspoon salt
1 teaspoon sugar

1 Bring the water to a boil in a medium pot, carefully add the tofu cake, reduce the heat and simmer for 4 minutes. Remove with a slotted spoon and drain. Alternatively, place the tofu in a steamer and steam for 4 minutes.
2 Mix all the Sauce ingredients well and set aside.
3 Place the garlic, ginger, and spring onions in a bowl. Pour the Sauce onto the garlic, ginger and spring onions and blend well. Place the tofu in the center of a small serving dish. Make 4 cuts across the top of the tofu in both directions, cutting no more than halfway deep. Drizzle the Sauce mixture evenly over the tofu and serve.

Serves 4
Preparation time: **10 mins**
Cooking time: **5 mins**

Stir-fried Lotus Root with Spring Onions

2 fresh lotus roots, about 250 g ($^1/_2$ lb) sliced into $^1/_4$-in ($^1/_2$-cm) pieces
1 tablespoon oil
2 spring onions, thinly sliced
1 teaspoon salt
$^1/_2$ teaspoon sugar (optional)
125 ml ($^1/_2$ cup) water
1 tablespoon toasted sesame seeds (optional)

1 Wash the lotus roots well and slice them crosswise into round pieces about $^1/_4$-in ($^1/_2$-cm) thick.
2 Heat the oil in a wok over high heat and when hot, stir-fry the lotus, spring onions, salt, and sugar for 2 to 3 minutes.
3 Pour in the water, cover the lid and reduce heat to medium, cooking for 5 minutes. Transfer to serving dish and garnish with toasted sesame seeds, if desired.

Serves 4
Preparation time: **20 mins**
Cooking time: **10 mins**

Home-style Fried Rice

Fried rice is probably the single most commonly prepared dish in kitchens of Asian homes, and it is rarely prepared from scratch. Instead, it utilizes leftover rice along with leftover vegetables, tofu, meat scraps, and other items to prepare a tasty hot meal that is quick and easy to cook, requiring no shopping. You may allow your culinary creativity to express itself freely when cooking fried rice at home, while also applying the "waste not, want not" philosophy of the Asian kitchen.

Assorted leftover ham, chicken, bacon, tofu and vegetables (except leafy greens), such as carrots, corn, mushrooms, peas, green beans, and onion
$1/4$ cup oil
3 to 4 cloves garlic, minced
1 chilli pepper, seeded and thinly sliced
1 large egg, lightly beaten
3 to 4 cups cooked rice, white or brown
2 to 3 spring onions, minced
1 teaspoon salt
1 teaspoon freshly ground black pepper

Serves 4
Preparation time: **15 mins**
Cooking time: **10 mins**

1 Dice all meat and vegetable leftovers into small pieces, then set aside in a bowl.
2 Heat oil in a wok over high heat. When hot, add the garlic, chilli, and leftovers and stir-fry quickly for about 1 minute.
3 Add the egg, stirring quickly to scramble. Add the cooked rice and continue to stir-fry until the rice and vegetables are well mixed, when the rice begins to brown, about 3 to 5 minutes.
4 Sprinkle on the spring onions, salt, and pepper, and continue to stir and turn for another 1 to 2 minutes. Transfer to serving dish, or to individual rice bowls.

The cooked rice should be dry and firm when preparing this dish; soggy rice does not work well in this recipe. If you have leftover meat such as stir-fried fish, they may be added along with the vegetables and tofu. A sprinkling of minced fresh coriander and a dusting of Sichuan Pepper-Salt Powder (page 3) on top of the finished dish provide some stimulating flavors that will add a lot of character.

Rice with Mixed Vegetables

This is a good way to use leftover rice, particularly brown rice, which does not get as soggy as white rice. You may use almost any combination of vegetables — such as turnip, bell peppers, cooked corn, fresh mushrooms, chopped cabbage, diced squash — to prepare this dish, and it may stand alone as a meal. This is a typical example of the pragmatic spirit of Asian homestyle cooking, which always regards leftovers as the foundation of another good meal.

10 dried black Chinese
  mushrooms
3 tablespoons oil
1 onion, sliced into
  crescents
3 to 4 cloves garlic,
  minced
3 to 4 slices fresh ginger,
  minced
2 carrots, diced
12 florets broccoli, stems
  peeled and diced
1 green bell pepper,
  diced
1 cup fresh or frozen
  peas
3 cups cooked rice, white
  or brown

Sauce
1 tablespoon soy sauce
1 teaspoon rice wine
$1/2$ teaspoon sugar
1 teaspoon salt
1 teaspoon sesame oil

1 Soak the dried black Chinese mushrooms for 15 minutes in hot water, drain and reserve $1/2$ cup of the liquid. Remove the stems. Squeeze excess moisture from the mushrooms and slice each cap into 4 to 6 strips.
2 Combine all the Sauce ingredients in a bowl and set aside.
3 Heat oil in a wok over high heat and stir-fry the mushrooms, onions, garlic, and ginger for 1 minute. Add the Sauce mixture, then add the carrots, broccoli, bell pepper, and peas. Stir-fry for 3 minutes.
4 Add cooked rice and continue to stir until all ingredients are well mixed, then add the mushroom water and mix through until well combined.
5 Reduce heat, cover with lid, and cook for 3 to 4 minutes, then transfer to serving platter.

Serves 4
Preparation time: 20 mins
Cooking time: 15 mins

Rice and Lentil Congee

190 g (1 cup) green
  lentils
120 g ($^1/_2$ cup)
  uncooked white or
  brown rice
2 liters (8 cups) water
1 teaspoon salt

Serves 4
Preparation time:
  3–5 hours
Cooking time: 2–3 hours

1 Wash the lentils and rice well, place in a large pot, and cover with the water. Soak for 3 to 5 hours, or overnight.
2 Bring the pot of water with the rice and lentils to a rolling boil, add salt, lower the heat, and skim off any foam and lentil skins that float to the surface. Cover partially to allow steam to escape, and simmer for 2 to 3 hours, or until rice and lentils are soft and tender. Stir occasionally to prevent sticking and add a little water as required to maintain fluid porridge consistency.
3 When cooked, turn off the heat and leave the pot covered on the stove until ready to serve. The cooked congee may be eaten as a staple grain with meals, just like ordinary rice.

You may prepare congee with a variety of other grains and pulses, using the same basic proportions as above. For example, use 60 g ($^1/_4$ cup) ordinary uncooked rice and 60 g ($^1/_4$ cup) uncooked wild rice, which gives the congee a unique nutty taste and extra nutritional value, or try red rice. You may also substitute red or yellow lentils for the green ones, or use soya beans or black-eye peas. It's helpful to soak the rice and beans overnight rather than just for a few hours, and always be sure to keep your eye on the pot while cooking to make sure the porridge does not become too dry.

Seasoned Rice and Lentil Congee

With the addition of a few seasoning, the basic Rice and Lentil Congee is elevated to a delicious one-pot dish that may be eaten as a meal in itself.

One portion Rice and
  Lentil Congee (above)
1 teaspoon sesame oil
$^1/_2$ teaspoon salt
$^1/_2$ teaspoon freshly
  ground black pepper
1 teaspoon minced
  spring onion

1 Place seasonings into each individual bowl.
2 Add a spoonful of hot congee to each bowl, stir well to blend the seasonings, then fill the bowls to the top with congee and stir to blend flavors.

Serves 4
Preparation time: **10 mins**
Cooking time: **10 mins**

Millet and Brown Rice Congee

Millet is the oldest grain on record as a staple cereal crop in China. Although it is rarely consumed any more in the West, millet remains one of the most beneficial of all grains for human health. It is also very easy to digest and it is the only grain that alkalizes rather than acidifies the stomach. Millet lends itself best to the preparation of congee and in this recipe it is combined with the hearty flavor and chewy texture of brown rice.

200 g (1 cup) uncooked brown rice
4 liters (16 cups) water
125 g ($^1/_2$ cup) uncooked millet
1 teaspoon salt

Seasoning
1 teaspoon sesame oil
$^1/_2$ teaspoon freshly ground black pepper
$^1/_2$ teaspoon salt
1 spring onion, minced

Serves 4
Preparation time: 5 mins
 + 3–5 hours soaking
Cooking time: 1$^1/_4$ hours

1 Wash and rinse the brown rice well, then place in a large pot and add the water. Set aside to soak for 3 to 5 hours, or overnight.
2 Bring the water and rice to a boil over high heat, then add the millet and salt. When water comes to a full boil, reduce the heat to medium-low, cover partially with lid to allow steam to escape and simmer until it reaches the consistency of porridge, about 1$^1/_4$ hours. Stir occasionally to prevent sticking and add water as needed if it gets too dry.
3 Turn off the heat and leave the pot covered until ready to serve.
4 Divide the Seasoning among individual serving bowls, spoon the congee on top and stir to blend the flavors.

Sweet Rice and Lentil Porridge

By adding a little sugar and spice to the basic Rice and Lentil Congee (page 10), you can enjoy a very easy-to-make dessert.

One portion of cooked Rice and Lentil Congee (page 10)
75 g ($^1/_2$ cup) raw cane sugar
Cinnamon stick or powder, and split vanilla bean or extract (both optional)

1 Follow the recipe for Rice and Lentil Congee. Either place the cinnamon stick and vanilla bean into the pot while cooking the Rice and Lentil Congee or place into individual serving bowls and stir to blend flavors.

Serves 4
Preparation time: 10 mins
Cooking time: 10 mins

Noodles in Vegetable Broth

3–4 liters (12–16 cups) water, to cook noodles

1¹/₂ liters (6 cups) water, with 1 teaspoon salt, to make vegetable broth

8–12 dried black Chinese mushrooms, soaked in 250 ml (1 cup) hot water

250 g (8 oz) dried or 500g (1lb) fresh wheat noodles

8 florets fresh broccoli, stems peeled, each cut into pieces

8 florets fresh cauliflower, stems peeled, each cut into pieces

1 large or 2 small heads bok choy, washed with leaves separated

Seasoning

2 spring onions, minced

4 teaspoons sesame oil

2 teaspoons sugar

2 teaspoons Sichuan pepper-salt powder (page 3)

Serves 4
Preparation time: **30 mins**
Cooking time: **30 mins**

1 Bring the water for the noodles and the vegetable broth to a boil over high heat in separate pots.

2 Drain mushrooms, adding the soaking water to the pot for the vegetable broth. Discard the mushroom stems and cut each mushroom in half.

3 Boil the noodles over high heat and cook until done, about 5 to 7 minutes for dried noodles (check the label for instructions), or about 30 seconds for fresh noodles. Drain the noodles and divide them among four serving bowls.

4 Add the mushrooms to the boiling salted water and simmer for 10 minutes. Add the broccoli and cauliflower and simmer for 2 more minutes, then add the bok choy leaves and simmer 1 more minute. Turn off the heat.

5 Divide the Seasoning among the bowls of noodles and mix to combine.

6 With a slotted spoon or chopsticks, distribute the cooked vegetables evenly among the four bowls of noodles, then ladle enough broth from the pot to fill each bowl. Serve hot.

This dish is usually prepared with ordinary Chinese wheat noodles, dried or fresh, but any sort of noodles, such as rice noodles or bean thread vermicelli can be used as long as you follow the cooking instructions on the package labels. And, of course, you may substitute any combination of vegetables that suits your tastes and nutritional requirements.

Sesame Noodles

The sauce may be blended to suit anyone's personal taste and virtually any type of wheat noodle may be used. Moreover, sesame is a rich source of vegetable protein, minerals and other vital nutrients.

3–4 liters (12–16 cups) water
250 g ($^1/_2$ lb) dried wheat noodles, or 500 g (1 lb)
  fresh noodles
150 g (5 oz) fresh mung beansprouts, washed
  and drained

Sauce
3 tablespoons sesame paste or tahini
1 teaspoon salt
1 teaspoon sugar
1 tablespoon soy sauce
1 teaspoon vinegar
1 teaspoon freshly ground black pepper
2 spring onions, minced

1 Bring the water to a rolling boil; do not add salt.
2 Add the noodles to the water and cook dried noodles according to package directions, or about 30 seconds for fresh noodles. Test to make sure they are tender before removing from the pot.
3 Drain noodles in a colander, rinse in cold water, drain and place in a large bowl.
4 Combine Sauce ingredients in a bowl and add the Sauce to the noodles. Toss well to mix thoroughly.
5 Place portions into individual serving bowls, garnish with beansprouts and serve.

For garnish, you may also use thinly shredded cucumber and carrot. For those who like it spicy, add 1 tablespoon of chilli sauce or 1 teaspoon of crushed red pepper to the Sauce, or sprinkle crushed red pepper onto individual servings.

Serves 4
Preparation time: **15 mins**
Cooking time: **30 mins**

Vegetable and Tofu Soup

6 cups (1 ½ liters) water
2 teaspoons salt
8–12 dried black Chinese mushrooms, soaked in hot
water and drained
150 g (5 oz) fresh spinach, watercress, bok choy or
similar greens
200 g (7 oz) silken tofu, cut into cubes
5 slices ginger, thinly shredded
2 sprig fresh coriander leaves (cilantro), cut into short
lengths

1 Bring the water to the boil over high heat in a large pot, then add salt.
2 Cut and discard the tough stems from the mushrooms, then cut the large caps in half (if using small caps, leave them whole).
3 Wash and rinse the vegetables. Remove any tough or wilted stems, and separate the leaves.
4 Add the mushrooms to the boiling water, and let the water return to the boil, then add the tofu and ginger. Return to the boil over medium heat, cover, and simmer for about 20 minutes.
5 Add the vegetables and stir, return to the boil, then simmer for 2 more minutes.
6 Serve garnished with fresh coriander leaves (cilantro).

Adding a few dashes of sesame oil to this soup gives it a rich, nutty aromatic flavor. Other popular table condiments for this soup are freshly ground black pepper, Sichuan pepper-salt powder (page 3) and various chilli sauces. You may also use other kinds of vegetables to make this soup. Broccoli is quite good (but be sure to peel the stems, which are bitter), or try cauliflower, cabbage, turnip and beansprouts.

Serves 4
Preparation time: **20 mins**
Cooking time: **30 mins**

Steamed Whole Fish with Fragrant Sauce

1 whole fresh fish such as sea bass, perch, snapper, pomfret or trout, about 650 g (1 1/2 lb)
1 small carrot
4 slices garlic, minced
3 spring onions, thinly sliced
1/2 teaspoon freshly ground black pepper

Sauce
1 tablespoon soy sauce
1 tablespoon rice wine
1 teaspoon sesame oil
1 teaspoon sugar
1/2 teaspoon salt
1 teaspoon cornstarch dissolved in 2 tablespoons water

Serves 4
Preparation time: 30 mins
Cooking time: 15 mins

1 Prepare a steamer with rack and bring the water to a boil over high heat.

2 Scale and gut the fish, or have this done at the market, but leave the head, tail and fins on. With a sharp knife, make 3 diagonal cuts into the flesh on both sides of the fish. Sprinkle with wine inside and out. Cut a small carrot in half lengthwise, place the pieces across a steaming plate, and set the fish on top, so that the steam may circulate under the fish. Or use 2 thick spring onions for this purpose.

3 Place the ginger slices inside the fish.

4 Mix the Sauce ingredients in a small pan and stir over low heat until Sauce is well blended and thickens. Turn off heat and leave on stove.

5 Place the plate with the fish on the rack in the steamer, cover tightly and steam over high heat for 10 minutes (12 minutes for larger fish). If the lid is not tight, put something heavy on top of it to keep the steam from escaping.

6 Remove plate from steamer, then carefully transfer the fish to a serving dish, using two spatulas so that it does not fall apart.

7 Dust the fish lightly with salt, then spread the spring onions slivers evenly over the fish. Reheat the sauce until it boils, then drizzle it slowly over the spring onions. Dust with freshly ground black pepper and serve.

Another way of cooking this dish is to prepare it exactly as above, but instead of pouring a sauce over the steamed fish, drizzle 60 ml (1/4 cup) of very hot oil over it (heat the oil in a small pan until it smokes). This wilts the spring onions and sizzles the skin of the fish. You may also substitute thinly sliced fresh coriander leaves (cilantro) for the spring onions.

Red-braised Fish Steak

Red-braising is a traditional Chinese method of cooking meat, poultry and seafood. After searing the item to be cooked in hot oil, a fragrant sauce containing some sugar and soy sauce is poured over it, then the pan is covered and the food allowed to braise for a while. The characteristic dark red sheen is produced by the fusion of soy sauce, sugar and fat. Red braising is an excellent way to cook deep-water fish steaks or fillets.

650 g (1$^{1}/_{2}$ lbs) fresh fish steaks or fillets (tuna, halibut, seabass, swordfish or any other firm-fleshed, deep-water fish), cut about $^{3}/_{4}$ in (1$^{1}/_{2}$ cm) thick
1 teaspoon salt
$^{1}/_{4}$ teaspoon pepper
2 spring onions, cut into short lengths

Sauce
2 tablespoons soy sauce
2 tablespoons rice wine
1 teaspoon sugar
1 teaspoon sesame oil
$^{1}/_{2}$ teaspoon vinegar
1 tablespoon freshly grated ginger

Serves 4
Preparation time: **15 mins**
Cooking time: **10 mins**

1 Combine the Sauce ingredients and set aside.
2 Rinse the fish and pat dry with paper towels, then sprinkle both sides with salt and pepper.
3 Heat a skillet or shallow wok over medium heat and rub the entire inside surface with a piece of fresh ginger (this helps prevent sticking). Add the oil.
4 When the oil is hot, place the steaks or fillets in the pan and fry for 2 minutes on each side. Gently shake the pan to help prevent sticking.
5 Pour the Sauce over the fish. Gently shake the pan to blend and distribute the sauce evenly, then braise without a lid for 1 to 2 minutes.
6 Turn the fish, toss in the spring onions and shake the pan. Braise for 2 more minutes and transfer to a serving dish.

For a spicier meal, add 1 tablespoon of chilli paste to the sauce, or dust the cooked fish lightly with ground Sichuan pepper (page 2). If desired, garnish with minced coriander leaves (cilantro), which goes very well with most seafood dishes.

Fish Stir-fried with Black Beans and Pepper

You may use any type of firm-fleshed, salt water fish for this recipe — such as tuna, halibut, snapper, sea bass, or swordfish. Different types of fish cook at slightly different rates, and the size of the pieces also influence the cooking time — so be careful not to overcook, as that will make the fish tough. This dish may be garnished with minced fresh coriander leaves (cilantro).

650 g (1 $^1/_2$ lb) fish
  steaks or fillets
3 tablespoons oil
3–4 cloves garlic,
  minced
1 $^1/_2$ to 2 tablespoons
  black bean paste
6 spring onions, cut
  into sections
1 teaspoon sugar
1 teaspoon coarsely
  ground black pepper
2 sprigs fresh coriander
  leaves (cilantro),
  minced, as garnish
  (optional)

Marinade
2 tablespoons rice wine
1 teaspoon sesame oil
3 tablespoons fresh
  ginger, minced

1 Cut the fish into bite-sized chunks. If using steaks, remove bones. Place fish in a mixing bowl.
2 Mix the Marinade ingredients, pour over fish, and turn to coat the fish evenly. Cover and set aside to marinate for about 30 minutes.
3 Heat the oil in a wok over high heat, and add the marinated fish and garlic. Stir-fry for 1 to 2 minutes, until fish changes color. Add the black bean paste and continue to cook for another 1 to 2 minutes.
4 Add the spring onions, sugar, and coarsely ground black pepper, stirring for 1 more minute to blend the flavors. Transfer to a serving dish.

Serves 4
Preparation time: 30 mins
Cooking time: 5 mins

Garlic Chilli Prawns

500 g (1 lb) fresh prawns, shelled and deveined
3–5 dried red chillies
2 tablespoons oil
6 cloves garlic, smashed
6 slices ginger, cut into fine shreds
2–3 tablespoons bottled chilli sauce (preferably garlic
    chilli sauce)
3 spring onions, cut into sections

Marinade
2 tablespoons rice wine
1 teaspoon sesame oil
1 teaspoon sugar
$^{1}/_{2}$ teaspoon cornstarch mixed with 1 tablespoon water

Sauce
1 tablespoon rice wine
1 teaspoon soy sauce
1 tablespoon tomato ketchup
1 teaspoon salt

1 Mix the Marinade ingredients in a bowl, then add
the prawns and toss to coat. Set aside to marinate for
20 minutes in the refrigerator.
2 Combine all the Sauce ingredients in a bowl and set
aside.
3 Cut the seeded dried chillies lengthwise.
4 Heat the oil in a wok over high heat, then add the
chillies and let them scorch.
5 Add the prawns, garlic and ginger and stir-fry quickly
until the prawns turn pink and the flesh becomes
firm, 1 to 2 minutes.
6 Add the chilli sauce and stir to blend, then add the
spring onions and the Sauce mixture. Cook for another
1 to 2 minutes, then transfer to a platter and serve.

> *Chilli sauce is a blend of chilli and water, seasoned in salt,
> sugar, garlic and vinegar. It is not thick and has a sweet
> and sour taste and is available in bottle in food stores.*

Serves 4
Preparation time: **20 mins**
Cooking time: **5 mins**

Chilli Chicken

Tender chunks of marinated chicken breast are swiftly stir-fried with chilli and other seasonings to create this enduringly popular homestyle poultry dish, which may be prepared and cooked in less than twenty minutes. Along with rice and some stir-fried vegetables, this dish may serve as the main course for a simple, but delicious meal that appeals equally to adults and children. Adjusting the amount of chilli paste easily regulates the "temperature" of the chilli taste.

500 g (1 lb) boneless chicken breast, skinned and cut into bite-sized chunks
4–6 red chillies, fresh or dried
3 tablespoons oil
1–2 tablespoons chilli paste
2–3 spring onions, thinly sliced

Marinade
2 tablespoons rice wine
1 tablespoon soy sauce
1 1/2 tablespoons sugar
1 teaspoon sesame oil
1 teaspoon cornstarch
2 tablespoons garlic, minced
2 tablespoons fresh ginger, minced

Sauce
2 tablespoons rice wine
1 tablespoon water
1 teaspoon soy sauce
1 teaspoon salt
1 teaspoon sesame oil

Serves 4
Preparation time: **10 mins**
Cooking time: **7 mins**

1 Combine all the Marinade ingredients, mixing well. Place the chicken chunks in a bowl, then pour the Marinade over the chicken, coating the pieces well. Set aside to marinate for 20 to 30 minutes.
2 While the chicken is marinating, combine the Sauce ingredients in a small bowl and set aside.
3 Cut the chillies lengthwise and scrape away the seeds and white membranes.
4 Heat the oil in a wok over high heat and add the chillies. When chillies are scorched and smoking, add the marinated chicken and quickly stir-fry for 2 minutes. Add the chilli paste and cook for another 1 minute.
5 Reduce the heat to low and stir in the Sauce. Cover wok with a lid and simmer for 2 to 3 minutes. Remove from the heat, stir in the spring onions and transfer to a serving dish.

Chilli paste is a blend of ground, fresh or dried chillies. Not to be confused with chilli sauce, it is thicker and spicier, and is sometimes fermented to further enhance its flavor. It is sold mainly in jars and is widely available in food stores. To add some color and flavor to this dish, you may add 1/2 cup fresh or frozen green peas, diced carrots and diced red or green bell peppers. These should be added right after the chilli paste, but before the sauce. For extra zest, garnish the dish with a generous sprinkling of minced fresh coriander leaves (cilantro).

Five-spice Chicken with Garlic and Spring Onions

You can also add 60 g ($^1/_2$ cup) fresh or frozen green peas after stir-frying the chicken for a minute or two. A sprinkling of minced fresh coriander leaves on the finished dish goes very well with these flavors.

350 g (12 oz) chicken breast, cubed
3 tablespoons sesame oil
5–6 cloves garlic, minced
2 spring onions, cut into sections

Marinade
2 tablespoons rice wine
1 tablespoon soy sauce
1 teaspoon sesame oil
1 teaspoon sugar
$^1/_2$ teaspoon salt
2 teaspoons five spice powder
1 teaspoon cornstarch dissolved in 1 table-spoon water

1 Place the chicken in a bowl with the Marinade ingredients, stirring to coat the chicken well. Set aside for 15 to 20 minutes.
2 Drain the Marinade, reserving all the liquid.
3 Heat the sesame oil over high heat, and when hot, add the garlic and chicken, and stir-fry for 3 to 4 minutes, then add the reserved Marinade and spring onions and cook for another 2 minutes. Transfer to a serving dish.

Serves 4
Preparation time: **20 mins**
Cooking time: **6 mins**

Red-braised Pork with Orange Peel

You'll find this dish served in almost all Chinese night markets. Home cooks pride themselves on creating their own original blend of seasonings for this dish, which is one of the richest on the entire Chinese menu. Minced fresh coriander leaves (cilantro) makes an excellent garnish for braised pork shank, because its sharp, fresh taste balances nicely with the rich, sweet flavors of the pork. You may reserve the remaining braising sauce in a jar and store it in the refrigerator for use as a flavoring sauce for stir-fry cooking, or to braise other foods, such as tofu or fish.

1 whole pork shank, about 1 1/2 kg (3 lb)
250 ml (1 cup) soy sauce
500 ml (2 cups) rice wine
500 ml (2 cups) water
125 ml (1/2 cup) vinegar
75 g sugar (1/2 cup), preferably rock crystal sugar
2 in (5 cm) fresh ginger, thinly sliced
6 spring onions, cut into sections
Peel of one whole fresh orange
1 stick cinnamon, broken into 2 or 3 pieces
1 teaspoon Sichuan peppercorns
2 whole star anise
250 g (1/2 lb) fresh spinach, blanched

1 Fill a large stockpot about two-thirds full of water and bring to a rolling boil. Place the pork shank into the water and bring to a boil, then pour all the water out into the sink, leaving the shank in the pot.

2 Add the remaining ingredients except the spinach to the pot and place pot over high heat and bring the contents to a boil, then reduce heat to medium, cover with lid and simmer for about 3 hours, turning the shank over occasionally. After 2 hours, reduce heat to medium–low, and check from time to time to make sure that the sauce has not evaporated too much. If the level of sauce does not cover at least one-third of the shank, add another cup or two of rice wine mixed in equal portions with water

3 When done, turn off heat, and let pot stand, covered, on stove until ready to serve.

4 To serve, lay a bed of blanched spinach on a platter, then transfer the whole shank onto the spinach. Use a knife and fork to break the shank apart, then drizzle some of the braising sauce over it.

Serves 4
Preparation time: **15 mins**
Cooking time: **3 hours**

Braised Fresh Pumpkin

This is one of the simplest dishes of all to cook, relying entirely on the unadorned rich flavor of pumpkin, which blossoms when allowed to cook in its own juices. Try to select sweet mature pumpkins for this dish. This is a vegetable dish that most children like to eat. It is a popular choice for family meals. You may experiment with different flavors, such as adding a cinnamon stick, a sliced vanilla bean or some sliced ginger root to the pot along with the sugar and salt. The finished dish may also be garnished with minced spring onions.

3 tablespoons oil
1 kg (2 lbs) fresh pumpkin, peeled and seeded, cut into bite-sized chunks
$^1/_2$ to 1 tablespoon sugar
1 teaspoon salt
125 ml ($^1/_2$ cup) water

1 Heat the oil in a large stockpot over medium-low heat. Add the pumpkin and cook, stirring occasionally, until all the pumpkin is coated with oil and begins to soften.
2 Add sugar, salt and water and cover the pot. Reduce the heat to low and cook for about 20 minutes, or until tender, stirring occasionally to prevent sticking. Remove from the heat and serve hot or at room temperature.

Serves 4
Preparation time: **10 mins**
Cooking time: **30 mins**

Spinach Stir-fried with Garlic

350 g (12 oz) fresh
spinach, stemmed, or
Chinese peashoots
(*dou miao*)
2 tablespoons oil
$^1/_2$ teaspoon salt
3–5 cloves garlic, thinly
sliced

Serves 4
Preparation time: **10 mins**
Cooking time: **2 mins**

1 Wash and rinse the spinach well, then place in a
colander to drain.
2 Heat oil in a wok over high heat and add the salt.
3 Add the sliced garlic and the spinach, and turn carefully with a spatula to coat all the leaves with oil. Stir-
fry for about 1 minute, or until all the leaves
are wilted and have turned dark green. Transfer
immediately to serving dish.

*Chinese mustard greens or broccoli rabe are also ideal
for this dish. Make sure that the vegetables are young
and tender; trim the ends of the stems, and cut into
bite-sized pieces.*

Broccoli Stir-fried with Ginger and Onion

650 g (1¹/₂ lb) fresh
  broccoli
3 tablespoons oil
6 slices fresh ginger,
  finely cut into shreds
1 onion, cut into
  crescents
1 tablespoon rice wine
  mixed with 1 teaspoon
  water
¹/₂ teaspoon salt

Serves 4
Preparation time: **15 mins**
Cooking time: **5 mins**

1 Cut the broccoli florets from the main stem, so that each floret retains its own stalk. Peel the tough skin from the stalks below the florets with a sharp paring knife. Cut the stalks into bite-sized pieces.

2 Heat the oil in a wok over medium heat and when hot, stir in the broccoli and ginger and stir-fry about 1 minute, or until all the broccoli has turned darker green. Add the onions and cook for 1 more minute.

3 Add the rice wine and water and cover tightly with a lid, steaming the broccoli for 1 to 2 minutes.

4 Removes lid, add salt, and stir to blend, then transfer to a serving dish.

Chinese Winter Melon Braised with Ginger

Winter melon has always been a favourite Chinese food, not only for its succulence and fresh flavor, but also for its cooling properties — which soothe the digestive system by counterbalancing the heating properties of meat, chilli, garlic, and other ingredients. Winter melon quickly absorbs the taste of whatever seasonings are added to it, so keep the flavorings to a minimum.

3 tablespoons oil
2 in (5 cm) fresh ginger, grated
1 kg (2 lb) winter melon, peeled, seeded and cut into bite-sized slices
1 teaspoon salt
1 tablespoon sugar
125 ml ($^1/_2$ cup) water

1 Heat the oil in a wok over high heat and stir-fry the ginger and winter melon. Continue stir-frying until all the winter melon is coated with oil and the surface begins to soften, 3 to 5 minutes.
2 Add the salt, sugar, and water. Cover the wok, reduce the heat to medium, and cook for about 15 minutes, or until thoroughly tender. Transfer to a serving plate.

Serves 4
Preparation time: **15 mins**
Cooking time: **20 mins**

Chinese Beansprout Salad
with Garlic Dressing

Most Chinese salads are made with vegetables that have been lightly blanched, and the range of ingredients used for salads in Chinese cuisine is much broader than those in the West. The actual word for salad courses in Chinese is *leng pan*, which simply means cold dish. This could refer to platters of cold cuts, tofu, beans, and anything else served cold. This recipe calls for two types of sprouts. Either one of the sprouts or both taste as good.

125 g ($^1/_4$ lb) fresh
  soy beansprouts, rinsed
125 g ($^1/_4$ lb) fresh mung
  beansprouts, rinsed
1 teaspoon salt
2 fresh spring onions,
  minced (optional)

Sauce
2 to 3 cloves garlic,
  minced
2 tablespoons soy sauce
1 tablespoon sesame oil
1 teaspoon sugar
$^1/_2$ teaspoon salt
$^1/_2$ teaspoon freshly
  ground black pepper
1 teaspoon vinegar

1 Mix together all the Sauce ingredients in a small bowl and set aside.

2 Bring a large pot of water to a rolling boil and add 1 teaspoon salt.

3 Blanch the soy bean sprouts and the mung beansprouts in the boiling water very briefly (about 5 seconds). Remove from pot and let it drain in a colander.

4 Run the blanched beansprouts under cold running water (5 seconds). Let it drain in a colander and set aside.

5 Mix the two kinds of sprouts together in a bowl, then add the Sauce and toss well. Garnish with minced spring onions, if desired.

Serves 4
Preparation time: **10 mins**
Cooking time: **2 mins**

Carrots and Black Chinese Mushrooms Stir-fried with Ginger

Black Chinese mushrooms have been a mainstay of Chinese cuisine for many centuries. Research has proven what Chinese cooks and herbalists have known since ancient times — that mushrooms give a powerful boost to the human immune system. The carrot, when combined with mushrooms, provides a crunchy counterpoint to the chewy texture of the mushrooms and contributes its own considerable nutritional value to this dish. For some extra color and variety, try adding half a cup of fresh or frozen green peas along with the carrots.

10–12 dried black
   Chinese mushrooms
2 carrots, washed, grated
   or thinly shredded
2 tablespoons oil
1 in (2$^1/_2$ cm) fresh
   ginger, thinly shredded
4 to 5 cloves garlic,
   minced
2 spring onions, minced

Sauce
2 tablespoons rice wine
2 tablespoons soy sauce
1 teaspoon sesame oil
1 teaspoon sugar
$^1/_2$ teaspoon salt

1 Soak dried mushrooms in hot water for 15 minutes, then drain, reserving the liquid. Remove the stems, then slice the caps very thinly.

2 Mix together all the Sauce ingredients in a small bowl and set aside.

3 Heat oil in a wok over medium heat, then add the mushrooms, ginger, and garlic together. Stir-fry for 2 minutes, then add the sauce and continue to stir-fry for 1 minute more.

4 Add the carrots and 80 ml ($^1/_3$ cup) of the mushroom water. Stir to blend, cover wok with lid, reduce heat to low, and cook for 3 to 4 minutes. Remove from heat, stir in the spring onions, transfer to a platter and serve.

Serves 4
Preparation time: **20 mins**
Cooking time: **10 mins**

Homestyle Red-braised Tofu

There are probably as many ways to prepare *hong shao* (red-braised) tofu, as there are cooks in China. This traditional method of cooking tofu, which by itself is a very bland food, allows the manifold flavors of the seasoning and sauce to penetrate the tofu, rendering this potent source of vegetable protein into a delicious dish. Each time you cook this dish, try a slightly different blend of flavors and proportions until you discover the style that best suits your taste.

5–6 dried black Chinese mushrooms
500 g (1 lb) firm tofu
3 tablespoons oil
2 dried red chillies, cut in half, seeded (optional)
4–5 large cloves garlic, smashed
6 slices ginger
1 whole star anise (optional)
6 spring onions, cut into sections

Sauce
3 tablespoons soy sauce
2 tablespoons rice wine
1 tablespoon sesame oil
1 tablespoon sugar
$1/2$ teaspoon salt
$1/2$ teaspoon freshly ground black pepper
1 teaspoon cornstarch dissolved in 125 ml ($1/2$ cup) water or chicken stock

1 Soak the mushrooms in warm water for about 20 minutes to soften, then drain. Remove and discard the stems, cut the caps in half and set aside.
2 Cut the tofu into bite-sized cubes. Place in colander to drain.
3 Combine all the Sauce ingredients in a bowl and set aside.
4 Heat the oil in a wok or large frying pan until hot, but not smoking. Add the chillies (if using) then the tofu, turning gently with a spatula until all the pieces are coated with oil and shaking the pan occasionally to prevent sticking. Fry until the tofu just begins to turn yellow but is not brown or crispy.
5 Add the mushrooms, garlic, ginger, star anise and half the spring onions and stir-fry gently for 1–2 minutes.
6 Add the Sauce and stir carefully to blend. Cover the wok, lower the heat and braise for 5–6 minutes, adding a few tablespoons of water if the Sauce becomes too dry.
7 Add the remaining spring onions to the wok and transfer to a serving dish.

Serves 4
Preparation time: **15 mins**
Cooking time: **15 mins**

Stir-fried Shredded Potatoes

Like chillies and tomatoes, white potatoes were introduced to China from the West, as reflected in the Chinese word, *yang yu*, which means "foreign taro." But like virtually all forms of food brought to China, the Chinese have applied their own culinary genius to the preparation of potatoes, which they neither deep-fry like the French, nor bake like the Americans. Instead of five spice powder, you could try dusting the finished dish with some Sichuan Pepper-Salt Powder (page 3).

4–5 medium-sized white
  potatoes
3 tablespoons oil
1 teaspoon sugar
1 teaspoon salt
$^1/_2$ teaspoon five spice
  powder
2 spring onions, minced
  (optional)

Serves 4
Preparation time: **10 mins**
Cooking time: **10 mins**

1 Wash the potatoes well but do not peel them. Using a grater, shred the potatoes into a bowl of cool salted water to keep them from turning brown.
2 Just before cooking, strain the shredded potatoes, but do not rinse, and place in a colander to drain.
3 Heat the oil in a wok over medium heat until hot but not smoking.
4 Add the potatoes and stir-fry, then add the sugar, salt, and five spice powder. Continue to cook over medium heat for 8 to 10 minutes, or until firm and tender. Add enough water as needed during cooking to prevent the shredded potato from sticking to the pan.
5 Transfer to a serving plate and sprinkle evenly with the minced spring onions.

Tofu, Green Beans, and Peanuts Stir-fried with Chilli and Garlic

This is a very typical Chinese homestyle dish, combining nourishing ingredients that are easily kept in stock in the kitchen and cooking them with a selection of stimulating seasonings that really help *xia fan* (get the rice down). For variety, add some diced carrots or green peas along with the green beans. If you have any leftovers, stir-fry it with leftover rice.

2 tablespoons oil
1 tablespoon sesame oil
300 g (10 oz) pressed or firm tofu, cut into cubes
2 to 4 sliced red chillies, seeded and then sliced
300 g (10 oz) green beans, strings removed
6–8 cloves garlic, minced
1 in (2¹/₂ cm) fresh ginger, minced
150 g (1 cup) unsalted peanuts, skins removed
2 to 3 spring onions, cut into sections

Sauce
1 tablespoon soy sauce
1 tablespoon rice wine
1 teaspoon sesame oil
1 teaspoon sugar
¹/₂ teaspoon salt

1 Mix the Sauce ingredients in a small bowl and set aside.

2 Heat the oils in a wok over medium heat and when hot, add the tofu and chili. Stir-fry for 1 minute, and add the green beans, garlic, and ginger, and stir-fry vigorously for 1 to 2 minutes more.

3 Add the peanuts and the Sauce mixture, and stir-fry for 2 minutes.

4 Stir in the spring onions, then transfer to a serving dish.

Serves 4
Preparation time: **20 mins**
Cooking time: **5 mins**

Spinach and Bean Thread Salad

This is a classic Chinese *leng pan* (cold dish), in which briefly poached ingredients are tossed in a strongly seasoned sauce. A dish like this usually appears on the table first, to serve as a *kai wei* (stomach opener), or appetizer or as a *jiu cai* (wine food), or hors d'oeuvres). There are many variations of this dish, but the one given here is a tried-and-true favorite of the ages.

250 g ($^1/_2$ lb) fresh
  spinach, washed and
  drained
1 small package (100g
  or $3^1/_2$ oz) dried bean
  thread vermicelli (tang
  hoon)
2 tablespoons garlic,
  minced

Sauce
1 tablespoon soy sauce
1 teaspoon sesame oil
$^1/_2$ teaspoon vinegar
1 teaspoon sugar
$^1/_2$ teaspoon salt
$^1/_2$ teaspoon freshly
  ground black pepper
1 tablespoon wasabi

Serves 4
Preparation time: **10 mins**
Cooking time: **5 mins**

1 Bring a large pot of water to the boil at high heat, add the spinach and allow the water to return to the boil, about 2 minutes. Immediately remove the spinach to a colander and reserve the boiling water. Rinse under cool water and set aside to drain.
2 Mix all the Sauce ingredients in a small bowl and set aside.
3 Soak the dried bean threads in cool water for a few minutes, then squeeze them dry by hand, and drop them into the reserved boiling water. Simmer for 2–3 minutes, then drain and set aside (do not rinse in cool water).
4 Lightly squeeze the spinach to remove any excess water, then place on a cutting board and cut into 2-in (5-cm) pieces. Do the same with the bean threads.
5 Place the spinach and bean threads in a large bowl, add the garlic and the Sauce, and toss until the spinach and bean threads are well mixed and completely coated with the Sauce. Transfer to a serving dish and serve.

Adding some form of seaweed enhances the flavor and the nutritional value of this dish. If the seaweed requires cooking, poach it the same way you poached the spinach and bean threads, then cut it to a similar size. Some cooks like to garnish the finished dish with a sprinkling of minced spring onions.

Snow Peas and Mushrooms
Stir-fried with Ginger and Spring Onions

Snow peas are one of the favorite vegetables of Chinese cooks. Snow peas and mushrooms are a classic combination in Chinese cuisine because they harmonize the *yin* and *yang* qualities. This dish may be prepared with either fresh or dried mushrooms. If you like it hot, add a few fresh or dried chillies (cut lengthwise with seeds and fibers removed) to the oil before cooking the mushrooms, and let them scorch before adding the mushrooms. You may also prepare this dish exactly the same way with broccoli instead of snow peas but make sure that you peel the broccoli stalks first. Another variation in flavor is to add a whole star anise along with the mushrooms and ginger.

250 g ($^1/_2$ lb) fresh snow
  peas
20 dried black Chinese
  mushrooms
3 tablespoons oil
1 in (2$^1/_2$ cm) fresh
  ginger, minced
2 spring onions, cut
  into sections

Sauce
1$^1/_2$ tablespoons soy
  sauce
1$^1/_2$ tablespoons rice
  wine
1 teaspoon sugar
$^1/_2$ teaspoon salt
1 teaspoon sesame oil

Serves 4
Preparation time: **20 mins**
Cooking time: **5 mins**

1 Wash the snow peas, snap off the tips, and pull off the strings.

2 Wipe the mushrooms with a damp cloth to remove any grit, cut away stems, and cut in half, if large. If using dried black Chinese mushrooms, soak in hot water for 15 minutes and drain; trim away the stems and cut each cap into four slices.

3 Combine all the Sauce ingredients in a small bowl and set aside.

4 Heat 2 tablespoons oil in a wok over medium heat, add the snow peas, and stir-fry until they turn bright green, about 1 minute. Remove from the heat and set aside.

5 Heat remaining oil in wok and, when hot, add the mushrooms and ginger. Stir-fry about 2 minutes, add the Sauce mixture, and cook for 1 minute more.

6 Add the snow peas and the spring onions and stir-fry for 1 more minute. Transfer to a serving dish.

Red-braised Tofu Steak with Chilli Paste

Tofu has long been popular as a meat substitute in China, and has made a big impact in the West, especially when cooked with robust seasonings and fragrant sauces, in order to become palatable and earn its place on the dining table. You may use black bean paste instead of chilli sauce and try dusting the cooked steaks with Sichuan pepper-salt for a different taste. This recipe transforms tofu into a "steak" that satisfies as much as any filet mignon — and it's even easier to prepare.

2 cakes firm tofu (about 500 g or 1 lb)
4 tablespoons oil
4 cloves garlic, minced
1 tablespoon chilli paste
2 spring onions, cut into 1-in (2$^1/_2$-cm) sections

Sauce
1 tablespoon soy sauce
1 tablespoon rice wine
1 teaspoon sesame oil
1 teaspoon sugar
Salt and freshly ground black pepper to taste

Serves 4
Preparation time: 10 mins
Cooking time: 10 mins

1 Halve the tofu cakes horizontally to form 4 pieces. Gently press the tofu with paper towels to remove excess moisture. Set aside.
2 Mix all Sauce ingredients and set aside.
3 Heat the oil in a skillet over high heat until hot but not smoking. Place the tofu in the skillet, and shake the pan gently to prevent sticking. Cook for 2 to 3 minutes, turn carefully with a spatula, and cook the other side for 2 to 3 minutes.
4 Push steaks to side of skillet. Add the garlic and chilli paste, stir to blend the flavors and prevent sticking.
5 Add Sauce, shake the skillet well to mix all the ingredients, cover with lid, reduce heat to low and cook for 2 minutes. Add the spring onions, turn tofu over, and cook for 2 minutes. Transfer to a serving dish and season with a little salt and pepper.

Mixed Diced Vegetables

1 cup fresh or frozen green peas
2 tablespoons oil
250 g (8 oz) fresh or frozen corn kernels (about $1^1/_2$ cups)
2 medium-sized carrots, diced (about $1^1/_2$ cups)
1 large green bell pepper (capsicum), diced (about $1^1/_2$ cups)
1 large onion (white, yellow or red), diced (about $1^1/_2$ cups)
150 g (5 oz) fresh or frozen green beans, tops and tails removed, cut into short lengths (about $1^1/_4$ cups)
2 tablespoons minced fresh ginger
1 teaspoon Sichuan pepper-salt powder (page 3)

Sauce
1 tablespoon soy sauce
1 tablespoon water
1 teaspoon sugar
$^1/_2$ teaspoon salt
1 teaspoon sesame oil

1 Remove the green peas from their pods if using fresh peas, or defrost the peas if frozen.
2 Combine the Sauce ingredients in a small bowl and set aside.
3 Heat the oil in a wok and, when hot, stir-fry the corn, carrots, bell peppers, onions, green beans and ginger for 2 minutes.
4 Add the peas, and continue to cook for another 1–2 minutes.
5 Add the Sauce, reduce the heat and cook slowly for 3–4 minutes, then add the Sichuan pepper-salt powder and stir for 1 more minute to completely blend the flavors. Serve immediately.

Serves 4
Preparation time: **15 mins**
Cooking time: **10 mins**

Marinated Chinese Cucumber Salad

300 g (10 oz) baby
  cucumbers or gherkins
3 to 4 cloves garlic,
  peeled and crushed

Sauce
2 tablespoons soy sauce
1 tablespoon sesame oil
1 teaspoon vinegar
1 teaspoon sugar
$1/_2$ teaspoon salt
$1/_2$ teaspoon freshly
  ground black pepper

1 Wash cucumbers well, pat dry and place on cutting board. Use the side of a cleaver or large knife to press on the cucumbers so they crack open, then cut into 1-in ($2^1/_2$-cm) sections. Place in a large bowl and add the garlic.
2 Combine the Sauce ingredients and drizzle evenly over the cucumbers and garlic. Toss well to blend flavors.
3 Cover with plastic wrap and let it marinate in the refrigerator for 1 to 2 hours, or for 30 minutes at room temperature. Transfer to a smaller bowl and serve.

Serves 4
Preparation time: **10 mins**
Assembling time: **2 mins**

Chinese Homestyle Scrambled Eggs

6 large eggs
1 teaspoon salt
1 teaspoon freshly ground
  black pepper
1 teaspoon sugar
  (optional)
1 teaspoon soy sauce
1 onion, sliced into rings
3 tablespoons oil
3 ripe tomatoes (about
  375 g or $^3/_4$ lb), cut
  into wedges

1 In a large bowl, beat the eggs well, then add the salt, pepper, sugar, soy sauce, and onion. Continue beating until well blended.

2 Heat the oil in a wok over medium heat and when hot, add the beaten eggs. Scramble the egg mixture quickly with a spatula for 1 to 2 minutes, then add the tomatoes and continue to stir-fry until eggs are uniformly cooked and dry. Transfer to serving dish.

Serves 4
Preparation time: 5 mins
Cooking time: 5 mins

Chinese Cabbage and Tofu Skin
Stir-fried with Ginger

1 sheet dried tofu skin
(about 80 g or 3 oz),
soaked in water for
10 minutes, then
drained
350 g (12 oz) Chinese
cabbage
1 tablespoon sesame oil
2 tablespoons oil
4 slices fresh ginger,
thinly shredded

Sauce
1 tablespoon soy sauce
1 teaspoon vinegar
1 teaspoon rice wine
1 teaspoon sugar
1 teaspoon salt

Serves 4
Preparation time: **15 mins**
Cooking time: **10 mins**

1 Cut the tofu skin into 1 x 2-in ($2^1/_2$ x 5-cm) strips.
Cut the cabbage leaves to similar size.

2 Combine all the Sauce ingredients in a small bowl
and set aside.

3 Heat oil in wok over high heat until hot, but not
smoking.

4 Add the tofu skin and stir-fry for 1 minute. Add
the cabbage and ginger, and continue to stir-fry until
the cabbage is tender, about 3 to 4 minutes.

5 Add the Sauce mixture, reduce the heat to low, and
cook for 1 to 2 minutes. Transfer to a serving dish.

*For a touch of chilli flavor that does not overpower
the whole dish, cut 1 to 2 dried chillies lengthwise,
scrape away the seeds and fibers and add them to the
hot sesame oil before the tofu skin. A sprinkling of
Sichuan Pepper-Salt Powder (page 3) over the
finished dish, plus a handful of minced spring onions,
will also spice it up nicely without smothering the sub-
tle flavors of the main ingredients.*

Sichuan Eggplant Braised in Fragrant Sauce

Chinese cooks usually prepare eggplant with strong seasoning, simmered in richly flavored sauces. This makes these dishes an excellent accompaniment for rice and congee. Leftovers keep well overnight in the refrigerator and may be reheated the next day for lunch.

500g (1 lb) eggplants
   (preferably long Asian
   eggplants)
3 tablespoons oil
6 cloves garlic, minced
6 slices fresh ginger,
   minced
3 spring onions, minced
1 tablespoon chilli paste
4 tablespoons water

Sauce
2 tablespoons soy sauce
1 tablespoon rice wine
$1/2$ to 1 tablespoon sugar
1 teaspoon vinegar
$1/2$ teaspoon salt
1 teaspoon sesame oil

1 Halve eggplants lengthways, then cut each half into 2-in (5-cm) long pieces.

2 Combine all the Sauce ingredients in a small bowl and set aside.

3 Heat the oil in a wok over high heat and when hot, add the eggplant, garlic and ginger and stir-fry until the eggplant begins to soften, about 4 minutes.

4 Add the spring onions and chilli paste and cook for 2 minutes. Add the Sauce and stir to combine all the ingredients. Add water and cover. Reduce heat to low and cook for 5 to 6 minutes. Transfer to a serving dish.

Serves 4
Preparation time: **15 mins**
Cooking time: **35 mins**

Complete List of Recipes